NOMADS OF AMERICA
& OTHER POEMS

POEMS BY
DANNY WADE SHEFFIELD

authorHOUSE®

AuthorHouse™
1663 Liberty Drive
Bloomington, IN 47403
www.authorhouse.com
Phone: 1-800-839-8640

Published by AuthorHouse   04/27/2012

ISBN: 978-1-4685-7378-7 (sc)
ISBN: 978-1-4685-7376-3 (e)

Library of Congress Control Number: 2012905603

Dedicated to Papa, Mama, Tuddie, Daddy, Darrell Wayne,
Deveron Dane, John Thomas, & Alex & Bri, Patti

Contents

& Other Poems

Nomads of America

All sources are a wonderment
There is no specialization.
There are no constraints on the mind.
The intellect pursues all knowledge.
You do not focus on specificity.
There is no confined direction or source to
    subscribe to.

Discipline of action is vacant.
The void is filled with want.
Soaring dreams are possible.
Joined with the multiplicities of pleasure,
Want is strewn within the philosophies of
    man & woman.
You are shown your harvested thoughts,
in Thracean, and Greek philosopher's words,
    in <u>Maldoror.</u>
Each wonder of discovery and understanding
    molds you as
the brother of humanity and the slayer of
    humanity.

That Nomadic impulse beats in your chest.
You move on as do
The Nomads of America

Genesis

The snake,
Keen willow switch lashing your back,
A mixture,
baking hot sun and dust,
The scent of sweat
of animals, of burden.

Your teeth crush, your hands twist
Cane juice from a cylinder of sweetness.
Rough slicing edges of slender leaves
Brand your innocent arms.
Shadows mark your mottled skin.

Silently, You lie, stretched flat,
As iron shod hooves pound you
Into the cooling earth.

Free to roam the generating soil,
Your universe connects with
The roots of things.
Images are acerbic, bittersweet,
Caustic, entangling,
Frothy, frivolous,
Canopic.

Causes frequently evade you, but,
You incur hardening pubescent pleasure,
Compelling the pursuit of . . .
Of self-induced pain,
Of loss inflicted desire,
Of irrational liberating libations
Breaking polluted inhibitions,
Of positions, postures;
Among pronouncements of agony.

Laboring for birth,
Spasms curl
The brain stem
Into a twisted knot
Of existence.

Your roots stretch back
Until you feel the first murmur
Of the earth's heart.
You are the blood that pulses through the
    first tiny ventricle.
The sea is your home, the savanna, the
    forest,
the desert.
The air envelopes your forms, while the
    clouds cry upon your sweet faces.

Your hands flail the flesh from bones.

Your lips seek the suckling teat.
You live! You live!

The sap flows along your mighty trunk,
Your arms reach for the light with power,
The petals lift from your eyes and you
   greet
The reflected sun.

Somewhere the elliptic effects wash through
other veins.
Young children pull liquid from the earth
and soften it with lye,
Old women scrub clothes on ribbed metal
   boards,
Before calling the power of wind and sun.
The farmer lashes the beasts of burden
Toiling to turn the earth belly up.
The simple pleasure of wild grape juice
sweetly dribbles into the mouth of a babe;

The assault of furious bodies sweats the
   bed of skins;
Entanglements gravitate to least
   resistances.

The Dream God reaches into earth and
     embraces Death.
Manure feeds the roots, then slender songs
     warble
From mouths of the lost and left out.

Tangled within webs of pleasure and
     persistence,
Poets begin to sing:
Cantos & canticles,
Crosses & crutches,
Canons & Crap.

Art hides its beauty in darkened caves,
tiny lights only
Illumining the precise hand's eternal
     presence.
Shamanic paths connect the worlds.
You suffer! You suffer!

They say pleasure is pain. You are
     stretched on
The racks until all possibilities are
     exhausted. But still there is more!

You have absorbed the source.
You have emerged.
You have seen the light.
You have embraced darkness.
You have suckled the unclean & fed those
    with plenty.
You have bred with your own kind
and blown possibilities
into incestuous disproportion.
You have scattered your seed upon the earth
and burdened
Innocent Kingdoms with wars.
You have yet to sing your song and you make
    predictions
based on false assumptions.
You have divided that which was one body
    into two but still
there is unknown growth.

Endless possibilities occur as you absorb
the nutrient Fresh.
Expansion is your name.
The multiplicitous Connection is yours.
Honor! Courage! Despair!
The lexicon of Sadness. The Pantheons of
Joy. Humor. Ha!
The Phalanx of Triumph And Tragedy.
All yours.

The teat of existence lies clasped
within the circle of your
moistened lips.
Risen from Mother Earth, Mother's nipple
gives you that connection back. The
Father's seed gives you that impetuous
Lust.

Depression

Seasons bud green with leaf,
Then dry dusty with heat,
Pass into earth colored autumn,
Frosts lie
Dormant and brittle.

Banks write their loans,
Then foreclose and fail,
As the venturous and speculative
Fall through the cracks and jump from
    windows
In cities, leaving buildings vacant and
    boarded.
Merchants stock their shelves,
Fill the orders, give credit,
Then write off the destitute's account,
Before turning their faces from the
    gathering hordes.
Farmers footsteps trace a familiar
but ever-changing track.
Walking the furrowed fields,
Men and Women holding slick leather reins
Slap the muscular haunches of the mules,
Heading them up the long and silent rows,
    until

The earth lifts around them, and darkens
    the sky, and they cover their faces,
    shut their eyes,
move on.
Oblivion, born from the manipulation of
    invisible monies
Scours the bowels of the land.

The Nomads of America, birthed on empty
    hope,
Bed with Despair, awaken to darkened days,
Rise and tread aimlessly across the land.

Depression is the word of their existence.
Deceit is the genesis of their fear.
Pain is the pace of their footsteps.
Hope is the dream left behind.
Hunger is the face of their children.
But,
Persistence is the nature of their quest.

Westward

We follow the sun.
Westward the sun
Drawing us onward.
Along the tracks the hobos,
On the roads the modern machines
Like covered wagons of old,
Piled high with beds and blankets,
Pots and pans, cheap sentimental treasures,
    special what-nots and delightful
    dainties,
Grandma's pain and Grandpa's anger. The
Young and Strong,
Creep along, hunkered down like beaten
    dogs.

Death rides the running boards.
Thirst becomes a companion with hunger.
Shame is the fabric of conversation with
    the lucky.
The journey eats the treasures.
The special and delightful are cast aside
    and turn back into Junk.
The load lightens but the road becomes
    longer and
The load becomes heavier.
Crosses too heavy to bear litter the side
    of the roads.

We are compelled.
We are commanded.
We do not know the order.
No one knows the order.
Still, we follow the sun.

We call on our gods, but are forsaken.
Guilt rides as our companion; we must be
*   guilty,*
Why else the swarm of locust,
The earth rising with the wind
Our dreams carried away;
Why else the factory doors
Closed in our faces, barred, while we,
*   still strong and Able*
Cry for work.
Oh Lord, why hast though forsaken us!

Everyone has a story, only the names are
*   different.*

Down by the riverside,
Near the train yard,
In the desert somewhere on Route 66,
A man who is a giant

Walks out of the darkness
Into the light.
Invited to sit, he hunkers by the fire.
Up in the Dakotas, he says,
I had me a scam, he says.
My partner and me wait
In alleys by restaurants.
We see someone looks prosperous, he says,
I grab holt and cover him with a blanket,
    he says.
My partner gits the money
Then runs like hell.
I let him go then, he says,
And run like hell, too, he says.
We score and buy bacon and flour
Then head for hobo jungle.
I'm frying the bacon in a can, he says,
My partner makes biscuits, he says.
Then a family comes out of the bushes.
A mother's eyes plead for her children.
Skinny like barnyard chickens, he says,
Twice as hungry, he says.
OK with us, we say, he says,

And the kids pull the half cooked bread
Off the tin, stretching it stuffing it
In their mouth, he says.
He shakes his head, looks down at his
    scarred shoes
His face grows wet and shiny as
the dark eats him up
again.
We know the cries.
We hear the wails
Keening through the night air.
We know the cries.
We cannot find the voices.

Some turn back,
Finding at the old place
A feather bed scattered
Like an abandoned nest in the wind.
Some laid their burdens down
To rise no more

✸

Seasons change.
Fruit trees flower.
The petals softly
Pillow the ground
Beneath spreading branches.
The fruit is taboo.
Knowledge is the special domain
of the Gods.

✸

We wonder about those
who rise squalling from cracker
jack, peanut filled kola
loins lactating breasts nippled in darker
    shamed flesh;
who rise from sow-bellied teat succulent
    corpulent lard
assed larceny running scared, seeking
    breath moist
burrows furred belly rousing thighs for
    hidden faces
pain, birth pain screaming translations;

who rocked with blast of shotgun a-bomb
    h-bomb clouds
reeking screeching science owls promising
    techno-
America new world Elvis temples Whitman
    whack-off
contests come suck belly full sleep;
who rise calling black bird wilderness
    split-tailed
cotillion dance of treacherous rapid breath
    hurling
rocks buck-shot clods lizard cotton boles
    green
fibrous bursting pricking stuffed mouths of
    cotton
moccasins;
who fanged dreams colic ferocious pneumatic
    throat belch
poison gas ovens remembered krypton gas
    eruptions
praying playing God on black tambourine
    skin drum
message unrecognized unknown melody singing
    Ayryan
praises speaking in tongues stuck to
    cleavened mouths

mouthing clovened hoof suppers;
who rise running vamped after seeking
    silent baby hued
nights star dimpled knees scarred with
    renaissance
wrecked needles plowed into turgid dust
    devils climbing
based red heavens;
who rise shortened breath thickening in
    nuclear aired
bomb shelters rocking and rolling tombs
    tuti-fruited
glistened commodities of copulated cows
    milk bitter
weeded in plain porcelain cupped bastards'
    palms;
who gypsy minded dance out of virginal
    vaginas Pope and
Christ blessed crying in one body blessed
    within
selves of torpid evil dreams demanding
    golden treasured
patience;

*who see mired feet in consumer US sucked
    deeper
everlastingly balled and chained broken
    with pitiless presence;
who see possibilities mad provoke
    masturbatory whipping fads
feeble detrimental to knowledge safety in
    lily whited
burial coffin cowing in cover dirt but
    premature
birthed.*

*we do not want to bridge
the desert rivers
we want to eat
the meat
the food
of being*

✷

and the second generation
out of the war
bastards flung across the land
blonde haired kids sickly with want
war bombs bursting and another born
on the dusty desert
just out of reach
below the parched playa
sweet water nourishing the scrub

and herds of deer stompin
cracked bottom of lakes
dried and bolted with heat

sand slides fashioning playgrounds
sun split lips
of children prowling the dumps
for chocolate cupcakes

molded to shrinking guts
and thickened tongues
and hollers of babies in the dark
bursting train windows
buckshot amid the booms
and roars of planes
screaming into the hillsides

out of the war
the brides folding delicate flowers
decorating the days
among the darkened memories
of sons and fathers

and they walk alone
shunning frosty slopes
searching the crevasses
for less putrid meat amid
the green stalk of spring

★

and the generation before again
the progeny of war
and the generation before
again the progeny of war
and the brothers and sons at their fathers
*   throats*
and the slashing of sabers against heated
*   flesh*
so suddenly frozen with the mud of the
*   fields*
beneath the plodding jackboots of hopeless
human misery dripping from bloodshot eyes
misery seeking mercy and mercy flown to
*   cover*
hiding with the beasts of the fields on the
*   stone*
slab of Isaac's sacrifice and the mournful
whip-o-will
songs of deafening blackness-blacker than
*   the tomb*

which was the start of it all, some thought
otherwise why the cool breeze of lush
    valleys
beckoning freely as a lovers touch, a poets
    song

crippling with its breath of false hope
fraud with hallelujahs fraught with

fraught with nomadic desire

ohh ohhh she sighs trembling with the gush
of broken placenta as the water born child
lands running
into the mist of morning paled from the
    embrace
of night whose clutches loosening retreats
before the burning brightness soothed only
    by the lick
of a protruding and tumescent tongue
    touched again
touched again she sighs she sighs as
    whipcord
muscles gather again for pleasure

or pain, the child

flower upon the valley floor past the hot
    sun's eye

plucking at the cool vision of the moon's
    gaze in a bright sky

and we gasped to see such delight as hers

bare and pure in that light swinging into
    her shadow

dragging hands slender with pain into her
    shadow

screaming her song of silence into her
    shadow

struggling with the weight of him into her
    shadow

as helpless and helpless and fascinated

we peel the animal skin back from our bones
laying in flagellated pose
we suffer to see to see
but again the slashing of sabers take our
    eyes
and the pain of salty tears torments our
    flesh
as she endures yet again the pleasure and
    pain
with her vision clouded by the rose color
of water streaming from the hot birth

forgive forgive she cries clutching at the
    passing shadows

clutching again at the delicate flower at
    her agonized fingertips she appears for
    an instant to be licking
the leaves of grass
in the dark of the moonlight

★

We know the boredom of comfort and stability. We know the uselessness of existence when we are embraced only by those elements. We know the excitement of balance when instability, uncertainty, the unexpected, and the unanticipated reign throughout our universe. When these things touch our lives, our soul awakens, the waters of creation gush forth and we find our tongues. We float in the cosmos and immerse ourselves in the cooling warmth of the earth as we traverse the paths of the Nomads of America.

Thank you for setting me free.

I knew the eruption of freedom with you. The song was again at my lips and in my dreams. I walked in the shadows of majic worlds and heard the stories of creatures there. I journeyed down long silver paths and caressed the lovely beauty of flowers underneath the glistening trees.

Thank you for my freedom.

I was the wave crushing the sands of the beaches and the rain falling on faces on chilled afternoons. I was the wind that caressed your bodies and lifted your dampened hair from your slender necks. I was the palm turned upward to catch your tears and the fingers intertwined with yours to provide you security.

Thank you for setting me free.

I was the sunny afternoon and the owl heavy in the tree above. I was the wolf you took to your nourishing nipple. I was the dream that shook your loins and your tender feet that stepped silently away. I was your eyes like serpentine stone and your ears like the curve of a spring willow.

Thank you for my freedom.

I was the storm that shook your foundations and the whirlwind that sucked at your quickening arousal. I was the sensuous lips on the curve of your neck and the fluttering hand upon the curve of your breast. I was the moistness between your thighs and the turbulent infant conceived. I was the mouth that devoured you and the breath upon which your fantasies rose. I was the rose petal upon your lips.

Thank you for setting me free.

I was the elements of shadow and fear in your soul. I was the cloudy and turbulent darkness that pursued your fears. I was the conflagration that roared in your veins and the ice that quenched your desires. I was the perfect season in one breath and the parchness of the desert in another. I was the hope just beyond your fingertips.

Thank you for my freedom.

I was your decadence and the redemption for your sorrow. I was the angel of mercy and the one who drained your lifeblood. I was the wound that would not heal and the never ending agony. I was the thorn that pierced your comforting heart and the sacrifice laid at your feet.

Thank you for setting me free.

I was the turmoil of your emotions and the fever of your spirit. I was the leader along rocky paths and the challenge of a steepening hill. I am your thoughts as you think of passion and your thoughts as you unleash your passion and I am your passion.

Thank you for my freedom.

I am the tinniest particle of moisture on
your tongue and the raindrop of your tears. I
am the tears of your stormy bodies as I fall
to the beckoning earth. I am the trickle of
water from the silent spring tumbling down
the rocky gorges and the rushing streams
running through the grassy meadows and I
am the deeper rivers that surge through the
painted lands and in my conjunctions with
the sea I am all the connections between the
Nomads of America.

I am
not of existence and not of futures and
    porkbellies and margins
not of existence and not of promises or
    promised lands
not of existence and not of milk and honeys

★

in the moments of tenderness
when the quilted fragrance of a lover's
   breath
hides the slashing blade of the never
   ending storm
and her touch of gentle forgetfulness
never quite pulls the curtain all the way
   down
and as we lie satiated
still the hunger fills our bones
and we rise facing the darkness
and wander into the night

in the moments of emotion
when tears slosh in our hearts of stone
there is at times a moan
that passes our clenched lips
as we pursue that rambling song
and feel the tiny hand clutched
between the stumped and ragged bones of
our own

in moments of fear
when the acrid stench of urine
moistens the loosely folded kacki
we think of the slaughter
and the gushing of blood
and hot scalding water
in huge tubs of iron

in moments of anger
when the tightened and quivering muscles
bunch with anticipated pain
the pleasure ripples through us
as the solid sound of flesh upon flesh
frees us like a frenzied fuck in the night

and we come home from the pacific paradises
and find we have fought the wrong wars
for the wrong side
for the wrong people
and we look the wrong way
and find we can never retrace our forgotten
footsteps

★

there was immediacy in death
but we were of the wind

never forgetting a languorous lounging
afternoon on the down
& hands gliding
firmly
slickly
along muscles taut as old leather
over hips tightened by the sun
& hands gliding
firmly
softly over strawberries and ivory
curves and a thin line of pubic hair

dark against light
light for the wind
but, we were, of the wind

as we stood looking into the weary eyes of
    a shadowy future
brine crystallized around glistening pores
    in wrinkled copper skin
children clutching the tattered legs of
    coveralls dressed in tattered legs of
    coveralls
crying salt tears down dusty faces dusty
    faces
and crying . . . and crying . . . !
our hearts as dry as the bone-white western
    wind
withering each day until at last only a
    wrinkled remnant remains
sucked dry of blood, lips smeared with
    despair and the heart
once again torn asunder like lava under
    smoking volcanoes
burning yes burning yes but hidden the
    strength
the weakness
the shame taking its toll, exacting its
    price

some days
we do tell our blood
we see them as glorious
we see them shining like in the old days
in the far dawns
as silently we watch
the dream lite up the eyes
as The Nomads of America
walk into a new dawn

The End
of
Nomads of America

& OTHER
POEMS

INVOCATION

Why is it oh lord
that I come on bended knee
beseeching you to intercede
with the demon clinging
tenaciously to my tormented soul?

Why is it oh my God
that I raise my voice
screaming in my supplication,
with torturous tongue
spewing entreaties?

Why is it exalted one
that I flay the hide
from my bleeding body,
my convulsing carcass
grinding into the ground?

Why is it oh most powerful
that tears stream
from my frightened eyes
falling frantically
upon the unforgiving dust?

And my prayers are not heard.
And my petitions are not acknowledged.
And my wounds are not anointed.
And the tears not washed from my face.

Is your power so weak and dismal?

Then I call for the demon to dictate,
For the demon to cast out these false beliefs,
For the demon to wipe away wasted hope,
For the demon to conquer my soul,
And salvation to be damned!

Dear Departed

I never sat next to a red wheel barrow
although I did take a lot of shit
from a lot of white-leggern checkens.
I ain't never gonna eat shit no more;
the barnyards a long time gone.

I departed that ding dong daddy Dumas
hospital,
that shot-gun shack by the ole Arkie River,
where I caught that wild bird
& saw that dead woman
when I peeked from beneath
the pink flannel blanket
the sun hazed through,
while I rode that old black baby carriage
with my brother,
whose bottle I stole ever chance I got.

I departed that cane-break
near the back gate to the river,
where mail boxes were nailed
to the ole pecan tree,
that grew by the lake,
that had a whirl pool,

that sucked my bamboo pote to its depths,
while I struggled in quicksand
& bullfrogs hollered in my ears.

I left that shot-gun shack,
where I ate my first snow ice-cream,
beside the smoke house
with the sub-machinegun hidden in it.

Yeah, I went to Pea Ridge,
listened to holy rollers
shouting & speaking in tongues,
near the bayou,
where I swam with the cottonmouth water moccasin,
& hunted pearls in muscle shells
that clung to the
bayou bottom of mud and rotted leaves;
went to Pea Ridge,
& hunted them ole mules
that always got out & stampeded
all over the country trampling cotton & corn,
till we herded them back
into the lot with the log barn
smack dab
in the middle of it.

I departed that place,
where I ate my first grapes
that grew wild in the woods,
where I shot them cows in the belly,
with my first spoke gun.

I traveled all the way then
to honey Lake,
which had no water in summer,
to turtle Mountain,
which was made all of stone.
I made friends there,
with two George Washingtons
between smoking liquid stones,
& they each had steel balls,
one black, the other red.
We ate fire grass,
jumped off coal bins,
examined young pussys in desert forts,
from where we could always hear
the cry of wild geese,
though they shouted
in the log cabin church
& prayed for God to stop me
from pissing the bed.

Behind a black curtain,
I burned God's word in the flames,
& they said Jesus
had my soul,
& Daddy detonated bombs
& clubbed my dog to death,
while I watched with by brothers
the blood run
from his nose
& his hind leg kick
spastic a few times.

Back I went to Pea Ridge,
made tomahawks,
got my head shaved bald,
ate half-moons in cotton fields,
ate crawdad tails,
& listened to the black panther
on the mountain side screaming.
Beside purple fighting flowers
I saw my brothers guts push out of him,
saw dead meat in piles by the road.

But, I found a crystal
treasure beneath the stones,
& I began to hear the music,
& the whole congregation laid hands on me,
& I didn't piss the bed no more.
God & I
were that close.

PAPA

I

Standing between his legs,
his arms
folded your small bones
to his chest.
His breath,
crisp as frosty autumn apple's
invited you to dream.

His hands, gnarled and broken
from the buckshot pellets
taped a rhythm
on his thigh,
as he danced the double back step
in broken old shoes,
cotton kakis crinkled softly
against his aging bones.

In his sweaty palms,
thin skinned with age,
there were coins he hid;
warm coins, half dollars
he gave to each grandchild
in secret, whispering,
"you're my favorite, you know."

II

Bullets were not for him.
He never spoke of war.
Before he died, in delirium
he talked with his younger brother
who had been dead
for seventy-three years,
head blown apart
from a buck-shot bulleted shotgun
one dark morning.

A Little Reminder of

Times & people not forgotten
Fresh breezes off your father's lake
His pond sprouting with cattails
Yellow & Red splashed birds
Singing into the air
Above the waters
Forever holding his essence

The Children

lately
walking

I have seen
the children
sitting
watching

the sun glimmering
on the sea

A LITTLE TIME

A little time
with something
Is better than a lifetime
of nothing

What Is?

what is this moistness
touching my cheeks?
what is this flower
with no fragrance?
what is this sun
hidden by clouds?
what is this night
with no stars shining?

is only a motherless child
looking for his past

Crumpled

by the barbed wire
& bleached fence posts
down the dusty road

he walked
away

Embraced

you gave me my first French kiss
you bought me my first prawn
you fed me my first avocado
you introduced me to sour cream on baked potato

you pulled me from the waters as I lay drowning
you paid $7 a week for a bed to lay my head on

the first time I went over 100 mph, you drove me
the first time I did a 360 slide on a bridge, you
    laughed and hugged me
the first time I swam Lake Temescal, you drove the
    back roads to take me there

you showed me how to dance
you sent your girlfriend to my bed
you picked me up when I had left home at 14
you grabbed the flashlight to bash our father's head
    in, pay for his miseries

& we floated the earth's seas and skies together
& in the end you held my hand and told me
you always wanted to be like me and I told you
I always wanted to be like you
& we embraced death

ODE TO BILLY BURNS

On days like this, sunny, warm and wonderful, Billy drops in on me. We recollect the early days, the baseball games on grass green and soft. I see him on days the sun shines clear and bright, standing by second base, glove outstretched, a particular look of anticipation, hope, and eagerness to his eyes before we lay down on the grass staring straight into the brightness of the sun until blackness is all we see and we wondered what world we were in. I trudge along the canal bank barefoot with him, mud squishing between our toes, picking the wriggling worms from beneath musty leaves, sliding them on our iron hooks, pitching them into the muddy water and waiting, without patience, beneath a cloudy sky, for the cork to sink, and with a yank of glee, pull the struggling perch from the deep, to capture it then, squirming like a tiny rainbow on the earth beside us. With our hands we caught it like now we catch the memory.

For many years now I have written these words in my mind to you, the recollections, whenever he has brought that green grass and sunshine personality to bear on me in my

*browsing. Did you want to hear it? In time I
told him, in time.*

*He was so awkward, that boy of yours, more
than me even in the darkened theatre, that
matinee afternoon we sat in front of the
screen, each of us sweating, clammy handed,
in the cool dark beneath the moving figures,
as we groped for female fingers for the
first time with love leading our hearts in
a thundering drum song. Afterward I laughed
and it was like the peal of a clear and
perfect bell, my voice, as it rang with the
exhilaration of affection and the triumph of
defeating the inner fear. Billy's voice rang
with mine and again it was the bright green
grass that shadowed our bodies as we lay
spread and open to the world, feeling that we
had conquered the mystery of women.*

*From that young awkwardness of body, he
grew into a solid-rocked oaken-hewed slab
of muscle and blood. Solid in body and mind
he stood by my side, and where before I led
him along the trails of life, he now carried
me over the rapids of the rivers of emotion
safely to the far bank, where he lay me on
the comforting grass and without words let
my orphan tears mingle with the water.*

*You know he came to me that night in the city
when I wanted to open my veins and watch
my blood mingle with the water of the bath
until the real world dreams were gone and the*

dark world dreams we held in our minds were the only reality. He was like a blonde god that night, eyes stormy as I imagined Thor's to be, but when he touched me, I knew what living was for, and after he spoke, I never had to ask the definition of love.

He has been the true friend. Clearly he speaks to me now, wiping from my memory the image of the plane tilted on its side in the center of a wide swath of charred blackness ringed by the brilliance and clarity of the spring grass.

BORN

Completely and completely
and again
again when
to the rectitude
revelation of rectitude
completely
again
again completely rectitude revealed
completely again rectitude completely
turned up turned
up completely again rectitude
up turned again completely
a going completely rectified
revealed completely
again agoing completely
rectified and revealed complete.

Blues

A little confused

sho nuff abused

Bluesong

I was born to violence
I was bred for pain
pounding out a decision
leaves me very little gain

Darker Than Black

the car so bright it's top cut off
turned round took off shot out to night
it found the lone dark boy in light
body so soft at once aloft
the voice tiny so small
silenced unheard after it's fall

the crowd gathered so loud in groups
the light down cast softly so mute
driver's lean face eyes flash sees brute
broken the legs in light which trooped
the son whose feet so quick did run
the son whose face without the sun

I want to be like you

I don't want to be strong
right
capable and confident
certain and assured
good honest fair and just
able clever or ingenious

I want to be like you!

LAZY

a **FLAGRANT**
VIOLATION
of
the **CONCEPT** of
ACTION

The Shell

black sand
clasps
the shell

bleached white
& broken

THE HUNT

the spider web
glinting in the afternoon sun
breaks across my darkened face
clings like magnetic silver threads
to my skin

as i climb the slate rock bank
the creek water
squishes from the foam in my shoes
squirts between my toes

my feet clinched
i squeeze the excess water
into silence

like the shadow of an oak
hicker nut, maple, elm

i move from trunk to trunk
the bark rough and connecting
my body to the tree's
stationary stillness

then my eye
catches the switch of a furred tail
catches the leaves fluttering like feathers
watches the branch sag slightly

slowly like the movement
of the praying mantis on the maple tree twig
i raise the ballistic barrel
& with breath halted & concentrated aim
i squeeze with measured pressure

now within the instant
silence is shattered
the corpse falls plumply downward
my feet rush quickened as my blood
across the softly dewed leaves

my hand grasps the warm blooded body
gun smoke and animal spoor mingle
with my sense of smell

turning with the quickness
and lightness of flight
i run captured in the completeness
of the hunt
the bushes and branches
whipping my body without hurt

the animal clutched by its tail
bounces against my body
as i, bound for home
among the familiar
trees and setting sun

I saw

I saw the smoke
Touch and move the moss flowers
Then move another bunch
The air floated left and right
In this night
The rain
Two hours of a gulley washer
Faded at Fayetteville
Then a rainbow curled the eastern sky
Then another
Two bars of color
Sprouting from the north horizon
Plunging into the south's

Then a drive into the countryside hills
A deer, eyes spotlighted in the headlights
A coon trotting by a mailbox
Mist, misty movements

And now
Almost a half-moon
Smiles from a hole in the clouds
And a star just above
To make a wish upon
In another pocket of blue space
And then of a sudden
Only wisps of mist floating
Among the two
With words flowing between
As the raindrops again
Start to sprinkle and sparkle

More Flowers

& little yellow blossoms are pretty
next to little red flowers
and poppy petals.

Lilacs are luscious
lavender and profuse &
Azaleas are passionate pink.
Pale ones are starting to pop.

Hyacinths are dropping their last golden blooms, foliage
        green now,
but Petunias—red and purple
delight the eyes again.

Flowers, flowers everywhere,
Like infatuation hovering
just under white clouds
beneath the blue, blue sky.

Dandelion Seeds
in the Wind

When she danced, I cried,
And when he danced, I cried once more.

The difference, majic & despair,
My soul sensitive as
Dandelion seeds in the wind.

When she danced, she cried,
and when he danced, she cried
once more.

The difference, majic & desperation,
Her soul sensitive as
Dandelion seeds in the wind.

SLUG

when I reached home
there was a moistness
like your kiss on my cheek
but it was only a baby slug
tiny and dark
which went down the drain.

The flower
I see
each morning
upon awakening
makes
My Heart Bloom
BEAUTIFULLY

Too much time with you

she said,
when i'm with you
time is forgotten.
when i'm with you
pleasure is paramount.

therefore,

we must
not see each other
so often.

Sometimes, the morning

you notice first
high branching trees
a pattern of twigs and leaves
intertwined nesting
among the limbs

if you sit long enough
three vultures
graceful as the floating spiderweb
in the light
in that same branching tree
spread their fluid wings
while extended talons
grip the bark

if you sit longer
a singular tree
distant but stark
can be seen through
the shadowed canopy
of limbs

in its imposition
the insect swarm
above the cone of green
glitters like tiny stars
as sunlight glistens
on wings like silver

if you sit even longer
lines of silk hang
among many trees
light running
up their lengths & down
like poured gold

where
the threads connect
the bark roughened runs vertical
darkened or grayed with lichen
or greened
with strangling ivy
so vibrant in its violent wounding

if you are still sitting
at twilight
the folk of this forest
scamper along limbs
to their nests
or fly in flitting
among the shades
some rise from their grassy beds
rolling their great bulk
to their knees
then onto
the clovened hooves
and spring away
leaving silence behind

if still you sit
with night falling
there the tremendous urge
to plant your body in the earth
struggles beneath the surface

if while lying & waiting
you hear
the mourning dove dancing
with the darkness
then you will emerge
brilliant
in crystal morning dew

And when you walk
home at night

after you pass,
the gypsies pull their cars off the road,
you have power over the gypsies,
and they guard for you
and the money collector,
dyed blond, black roots showing,
double parks by the junk yard.

And when you run to someone weeping,
as you come,
they carry the coffin slowly by,
the (flower) blossoms underfoot,
stones mark your passage,
eruptions like fountains,
flowing.

YOUR FACE

The moon at twilight,
The red morning sun,
Sparkling dew upon
Blades of green grass
In a mountain meadow
Is
Your face,
Filled with joy,
Resting in my heart.